The Darkening Trapeze

BOOKS BY LARRY LEVIS

Poetry

Wrecking Crew
The Afterlife
The Dollmaker's Ghost
Winter Stars
The Widening Spell of the Leaves
Elegy (Edited by Philip Levine)
The Selected Levis (Edited by David St. John)
The Darkening Trapeze: Last Poems (Edited by David St. John)

Prose

Black Freckles: Stories
The Gazer Within (Edited by James Marshall, Andrew Miller, and John Venable, with the assistance of Mary Flinn)

The Darkening Trapeze

last poems

LARRY LEVIS

Edited and with an Afterword by David St. John

Graywolf Press

This publication is made possible, in part, by the voters of Minnesota through a Minnesota State Arts Board Operating Support grant, thanks to a legislative appropriation from the arts and cultural heritage fund, and through a grant from the Wells Fargo Foundation Minnesota. Significant support has also been provided by Target, the McKnight Foundation, the Amazon Literary Partnership, and other generous contributions from foundations, corporations, and individuals. To these organizations and individuals we offer our heartfelt thanks.

Published by Graywolf Press
250 Third Avenue North, Suite 600
Minneapolis, Minnesota 55401

www.graywolfpress.org

Published in the United States of America

ISBN 978-1-55597-727-6

2 4 6 8 9 7 5 3 1
First Graywolf Printing, 2016

Library of Congress Control Number: 2015952175

Cover design: Jeenee Lee Design

Cover art: Francis Bacon, *Triptych,* 1970. Oil on canvas. National Gallery of Australia, Canberra. Purchased 1973. © The Estate of Francis Bacon. All rights reserved. DACS, London / ARS, NY 2015.

In memory of Philip Levine

CONTENTS

The Darkening Trapeze

I

A SINGING IN THE ROCKS

GOSSIP IN THE VILLAGE

I told no one, but the snows came, anyway.
They weren't even serious about it, at first.
Then, they seemed to say, if nothing happened,
Snow could say that, & almost perfectly.

The village slept in the gunmetal of its evening.
And there, through a thin dress once, I touched
A body so alive & eager I thought it must be
Someone else's soul. And though I was mistaken,

And though we parted, & the roads kept thawing between snows
In the first spring sun, & it was all, like spring,
Irrevocable, irony has made me thinner. Someday, weeks

From now, I will wake alone. My fate, I will think,
Will be to have no fate. I will feel suddenly hungry.

The morning will be bright, & wrong.

NEW YEAR'S EVE AT THE SANTA FE HOTEL, FRESNO, CALIFORNIA

for Bruce & Marsha

Smoke, laughter, & a bar whose solemn oak
Has outlasted worse times than my own . . .
In the ballroom of their last hotel, whole families
Of Basques had come again to dance, slowly,
Some austere polka nobody but Basques
Had ever seen, or learned. Once a year
I come back to this place, embrace friends,
And drink to what got lost in bad translation:
The town we tried to change, changed anyway.
The street we blocked off on a warm day
In 1970 is lined with cute
Boutiques, & that girl, once queen
Of her high-school prom, who two years later
Left to harvest sugarcane in Cuba,
Works late tonight, taking inventory:
So many belts, so many sandals sold.
Then jogging five miles home before she sleeps.

We drank Fundador late, & I went out
Alone in the cold New Year to find
No one on the street, no trains
Pausing in their own breath in the depot
Behind the hotel, no soldier, & no lovers
Either. What I heard & saw were a hundred
Sparrows gathering in one small tree,
Their throats full of some ridiculous
Joy or misery at being sparrows, winged,
Striped, & handicapped for life. I thought
That coming back here always showed me just
How much this place has changed; but no. The only

Real change is me. Now, when I sit
Across from two friends at a table, I am
Whatever's distant, snow beginning to fall
On the plains; a thief's fire. Someday I won't
Be home to anyone. Some days, it takes
Two hours of careful talk before I'm me
Again. I miss that talk, although I think
I'm right to be alone, in the gift of my
One life, listening to songs not made
For me, invented by no one I know, for luck,
For a winter night, for two friends who,
Some nights, some days, gave me everything.

LA STRADA

This life & no other. The flesh so innocent it walks along
The road, believing it, & ceases to be ours.

We're fate carrying a blown-out bicycle tire in one hand,

Flesh that has stepped out of its flesh,
Always ahead of ourselves, leaving the body behind us on the road.

Zampanò, what happens next? The clown is dead.
You still break chains across your chest though your heart's not in it,
Your audience is just two kids, & already there is

Snow in little crusted ridges, snow glazing cart tracks & furrows
Where you rest. And then what happens?

One day you get an earache. One day you can't breathe.
You notice the old nurse wears a girdle as she bends over you,

You remember the smell of Spanish rice from childhood,
An orphanage with scuffed linoleum on its floors.

You sit up suddenly, without knowing you have.
Your eyes are wide. You are stepping out of the flesh,
Because it now belongs to Zampanò, the Great.

Zampanò, I can't do all the talking for you. I can't go with you
Anymore. What happens next?

"Always what happens next, & then what happens after that.
It's like you think we're in a book for children. What happens next?
What does it look like is going to happen? It's a carnival.

It happens on the outskirts of a city made of light & distance.
And well, it's just my own opinion, but . . . I think
It's a pretty poor excuse for a carnival, torn tents, everything

Worn out. But I guess it has to go on anyhow. And I guess

Death will blow his little fucking trumpet."

CARTE DE L'ASSASSIN À M. ANDRÉ BRETON

It was Breton's remark after someone read it
Aloud to him that broke us up,

The remark, not the letter.

The letter was a madness with a system,
A pure system, Breton would say of it,

Pure because unafflicted by history,
A madness of childhood, handwritten.

I had to reconstruct it all this afternoon

By memory against the kind of chatter
That went on endlessly in the cafés

In those days. Now the style
Is to look as if you're molting in a cage,

Kids in leather like those sullen finches
From North Africa they sell in the pet shops now,

Who can't adapt to Paris. Or to anything.

Eh bien, at my age it's going to be more difficult
To adapt to what comes *after* Paris, since

What comes after it is nothing, & this,
I hasten to remind you, is a late spring night

On the Boulevard Saint-Michel, *this*
Is paradise! You can embrace it or you can sleep

Through it like a flowered wallpaper & pretend
You're still in, say, Omaha.

But the letter went like this:

Dear M. Breton,

Life has one sad wing,
And no claws.

Out of this lack,
It imagined the owl,

Though it did not tell it why.

Owls are as otherworldly
As they appear, they inhabit

Their shriek & the quiet
Glide of their wings,

They are the other world
That completed this one,

This one with its

Wars, amputations, bells
Above doors of shops,

A *Louis Quinze* chair in a window.

With only one wing & no claws,

It does no good
To know the owl's face

Is not a mask,

That it only looks like one,

That it is a thing
Without treachery becoming

A white target on a branch,

An innocence
Followed immediately by shame

In the quiet after the shot,
In the figures of birds rising

On the inlaid platinum
Of the antique Belgian 12-gauge double,

The little scene etched there
Above the trigger guard & makers' name,

Schwarz Frères, Luxembourg.

So that was childhood, he thinks,
Years later, a world within a world,

And the scratch of a pen
Against paper,

As he writes a letter?
He thinks he'll find it again,

If he keeps scratching at the paper,

He is convinced it will all
Be there, the boy, the owl

Turning its face to him

There, on the branch,
And finally he does not even

Need the pen or paper,
He looks for it in the tree-lined

Neighborhoods he passes
Driving around all night

In Dallas, in New Orleans,

When in fact it is the gun
He is looking for.

He loved the gun.

And now it is for sale
In a window.

Everything is for sale in a window.

And the woods float up the hill
As the owl glides above them at night

As it hunts perfectly
And without any apparent

Strain or effort.

Therefore, in accordance with
Your *avertissement* in a magazine

I ran across one day,
The rain outside the windows

Of the library, *L'Éphémère* I think
It was called, sitting there

With the others, pickpockets,
Drunks, unemployables, guys on the run

From something, all of us
Reading, reading, just reading

For hours, I hereby
Proclaim my willingness to be

Blindfolded, as you specify,
And spun around three times

By your assistants,

And at the busiest corner in Paris
You can think of, at noon,

And to fire a revolver of your selection,
Held at arm's length,

Randomly into the crowd

Until the chamber is as hot,
And as empty, as the skull

Of an owl.

        —

My employment for such a purpose
May be easily confirmed upon the receipt

Of a round-trip, first-class ticket
To Paris from the city postmarked

On this letter.

        Yours,

            Anonymous

Postscript: The nine-millimeter
Beretta is my weapon of preference,

If, however, your stipulation
Of a revolver is not negotiable,

A Smith & Wesson,
Appropriate caliber, please.

And, upon hearing its close,

Amidst the clatter of the little bar
Behind us there on Saint-Germain-des-Prés—

A place we didn't go to much, but it was
Out of the way, & most of us by then

Were getting on, were getting annoyed
By noise, by the long empty laughter in cafés,

By history, by . . . *everything*—
Breton exclaimed softly in that voice of his,

"America! Poor America!"

I'm sorry, but at the *time* . . . well,
        It seemed quite funny to us at the time.

THE WORM IN THE EAR

If peasants had written they would have ceased to be peasants. They remained peasants by remaining illiterate, & they only accomplished this against greater & greater odds as time passed by refusing to learn to read. In this way, they created the distance between themselves & anyone observing them. This is why, when Heidegger meditates upon a peasant he takes the peasant from a painting by van Gogh instead of any actual peasant he might have seen. And it takes Heidegger only a few sentences to forget the peasant & to think instead about a pair of boots in one of van Gogh's drawings.

Van Gogh, painting in those fields of stubble near Arles, set up his easel a few yards away from the peasant he began to sketch in. He was, by then, afraid to get too close to his subject. He was afraid of being ridiculed by the peasant he painted, by the small chorus of other peasants who might join in, who would begin to gather, as they had before, joking & jeering at him.

By that time van Gogh had already cut off his ear, but not, apparently, to get even with a prostitute. He did it because of the pain of Ménière's disease—they say now that was the reason—the excruciating pain that kept increasing, that came in the wake of the little Ménière's worm & its slow progress, day by day & week by week, into the canal of the ear & then, after that, into . . . into a pain I can't imagine. And of course it did no good to cut the ear off. It was too late. The worm was already deep inside the pink, lightless, inner tissues. Van Gogh would drink absinthe to kill the pain, which it sometimes did, although the by-product of absinthe, in the end, was the same as Ménière's, & van Gogh went mad from the worm which, having reached the end of the ear's canal, & having no other alternative, passed into the brain. He went mad just as absinthe addicts went mad from the distillation of wormwood, the principal ingredient used in absinthe. I don't know if he mailed the ear to the prostitute or not. The legend is full of bitterness & simplicity. Who knows? Maybe he imagined she might, someday, sew it back on. Maybe he had second thoughts, misgivings. Maybe he thought she could place it on her windowsill to listen for her, when she didn't want to listen anymore. Who is to say whether it was meant to comfort or to terrify?

As for the peasant, there is this one last thing to say for him. He refused to become a representation of a peasant. He was a peasant. He inhabited himself completely. The world would end, with or without him in it, & he would still be a peasant. The field would either be there or not be there. What difference could it possibly make?

That is what Heidegger envied, & what van Gogh painted.

And if that is it, if the soul becomes a peasant, & the peasant becomes only a representation of himself, & both remain illiterate, one within the other, walking together, the leaves flying, then the snows flying—then, since neither one of them can ever tell on or reveal the other, or ever have any reason to or any wish to, they have no excuses, no excuses for anything as the cold comes on.

Chin up? Ready?

TWELVE THIRTY ONE NINETEEN NINETY NINE

First Architect of the jungle & Author of pastel slums,
Patron Saint of rust,
You have become too famous to be read.

I let the book fall behind me until it becomes
A book again. Cloth, thread, & the infinite wood.

Don't worry. Don't worry.
In the future, everyone, simply *everyone,*
Will be hung in effigy.
The crêpe paper in the high-school gym will be
Black & pink & feathery,

Rainbow trout & a dog's tongue. In effigy. This,

For example, was written in memory of . . .

But of whom? Brecht gasping for air in the street?
Truman dancing alone with his daughter?

Goodbye, little century.
Goodbye, riderless black horse that trots
From one side of the street to the other,
Trying to find its way
Out of the parade.

Forgive me for saluting you
With a hand still cold, sweating,
And resembling, as I hold it up & a heavy sleep
Fills it, the body of someone

Curled in sleep as the procession passes.

Excuse me, but at the end of our complete belief,
Which is what you required of us, don't we deserve

A good belly laugh? Don't we deserve

A shout in the street?

And this confetti on which our history is being written,
Smaller & smaller, less clear every moment,

And subject to endless revision?

Under the circumstances, & because
It can imagine no other life, doesn't the hand,

Held up there for hours,

Deserve it?

No? *No* hunh? No.

A SINGING IN THE ROCKS

Quirai, the site of the Inquisition in the New World,

Is a cathedral of dust specks whirling in light now.

All the hallucinations of the nave, transept, the chalice with the sound
Of the wind inside it, the saint's relic like something obliterated

By the cries of another century—are there

To show how little they matter.

He rocks himself to sleep in this refusal to explain.

He naps in the empty spiderweb & is no more than its glistening
In the limbs of the apple tree—

How little they matter.

After driving all night I remember pulling over at dawn,
And climbing a low hill of twisted mesquite & a scattered

Outcropping of rocks gray in that light,

And hearing it there:

Dobro & steel guitar & the pinched, nasal twang of a country tenor,
A singing in the rocks though no one was there, & thinking

At first it was no more than the thin membrane & the cheap,

Inscrutable vision & brief psychosis that come in the wake
Of methamphetamine, a beige powder that smelled

Like wheat & was as silent, & was, for years, the only company

I ever had the pleasure of being completely alone with.

But the woman traveling with me heard it too, walking up the hill,
Waking to it there, so that she stopped & listened, but it was

As if she listened beyond it.

Even after we heard it there were the routine nights when she liked
To get quietly drunk on cheap vodka & think of her daughter—

Lymphoma a dead bloom in the woods, suspended leaves,

And how the nibbling of what was not yet pain when it began again
Was like disbelief flowing suddenly into the veins,

She was beginning to die, & to know it.

And so the singing, & the no one there, must have been
Different for her.

There was nothing we could do about it, & when the singing began
To grow fainter & cease, there was nothing we

Could do about that, either.

Not that a singing could have changed either one of us.

And the fact that we could not be changed seemed the brief meaning
Of what we listened to, there, until, after a while,

We could hear nothing but the unraveling sigh of traffic behind us

On the interstate. *"Fuck you,"* she said, & turned to walk down

A small path leading to the car, the parking lot, to a couple of

Weather-beaten public restrooms, the beige paint flaking off
The concrete & cement.

Beyond the valley I looked across there were mountains,
And beyond them, only another range of mountains,

And beyond them, another.

He is & is not the empty track of the fox,
And is & is not the edge of the wood that seems to be listening,
The paths disappearing again & again,

And the swirled snow making the darkness of the shop fronts

Visible, to show you how little they matter.

So say it & be done with the saying of it:

He waits & will wait forever in the delicate, small bones of the knight
Asleep in his luster, his armor, the glint of the swordblade at his side

Reflecting the raining sky & a life without the slightest hesitation.

He rejoices in pleasures too pure for this world.
He is the sore screech of the wheel in the addict's voice,

And disbelief itself under the summer stars.

And the tenor voice of the sax & the snow swirling on the city streets
To frame the unsayable, & mute the sayable.

And in the perpetual snow of syllables meant to praise him,
Nothing changes but his sex & his preoccupations, so that he becomes,

In time, the woman

With a birthmark & a puzzled expression on her face as she listens
To the clattering loom of voices in the asylum, listens

For the scrape of the keel on the sand & the gulls' cries.

If he is the saying, he is the obliteration of the saying,

And the sore screech of the wheel that outlives the addict.

They will say he is the saying & the finishing of the saying,
And that even the unsaying restores the beginning.

It isn't so, & the hawk caught in the boy's net

That I watched, later that day, had no sophistry about it, no guile.
Its choice was the tearing of itself to shreds.

So that, in an hour or so, it bled to death. And, therefore, no.
And therefore

He is the moment the trap springs give & something is snagged
For a last time in the cross-stitched mesh of the net.

So say that on a hill of twisted mesquite & a scattered outcropping
Of rocks gray in that first light,

He was the singing & the no one there,

Dobro & slide guitar & the pinched, nasal twang of a country tenor.

And a dust of snow, already, glimpsed suddenly in a furrow,
On a windowsill, on the frayed cuff of someone on a park bench

Staring intently at nothing, at passing traffic.

And therefore I say without the fear

That has been my faithful accomplice, & conniver corkscrewing

Through all my days until they resembleth the cracked glaze of frost
Already dissolved

By light, by the nothing all light is,

That in the moment after Dobro & slide guitar & the pinched note
Of defeat in her voice had ceased,

Something continued, unaccompanied, as I turned away from it,
And therefore,

He is the singing in the rocks & the no one there.

He is the pain & the frostbite in the melody.

　　——

There should be some third & final thing to say of him here, although
It should be said by someone else, leaning at four a.m.

On the scuffed black leatherette of a too-tall, out-of-fashion speaker,
Only the amp glowing on the dark stage of a country-rock bar

In Missouri, smoking & staring out at the empty dance floor,

And there isn't. And therefore:

　　——

What comes after, in the walking home alone forever, & the writing it
Out, is like the testimony of a witness, always imperfect, changing,

Until one is spent in the exhaustion of the music, in each twisted,

Unmemorized limb of mesquite scoring the blood-spattered
Hawk's screech of each note—no voice left in it & no accompaniment—

What comes after is the knowledge that

One is no longer part of it, & can no longer be part of it,

Who, with no one to answer to, passes the brown, indifferent grasses

In the winter months, the lascivious blooms that come on later, cock
Purple & blush pink, noticing them one moment, then looking away

Without focusing on anything in particular, unable to believe either
The chill of visitation or any lie the wind tells him—

Forgetting, & becoming,

Without the slightest awareness of it in that moment, another.

GHAZAL

Does exile begin at birth? I lived beside a wide river
For so long I stopped hearing it.

As when a glass shatters during an argument,
And we are secretly thrilled. . . . We wanted it to break.

Always something missing now in the cry of one bird,
Its wings flared against the wood.

Still, everything that is singular has a name:
Stone, song, trembling, waist, & snow. I remember how

My old psychiatrist would pinch his nose between
A thumb & forefinger, look up at me & sigh.

II

THE SPINE REMEMBERS WINGS

GHOST CONFEDERACY

They were the uncountable stars, the first time
We saw them, they were the glitter and the distance.
We were the swimming shapes of trees, that cast

Of shade extending over their tents. We hid
In ravines, but not to be one with nature.
We knew what being one with nature really meant.

And we were never the color-blind grasses,

We were never the pattern of the snake
Fading into the pattern of the leaves;
We were the empty clarity one glimpses

In water falling, in water spreading into
A thin white veil on what is never there,
The moment clear and empty as a heaven

Someone has just swept clean of any meaning.

If minié ball or cannon fire had a meaning,
We would have had maybe thirty seconds left
Of heaven to pin the right leaves back on trees

In summer and reattach the amputated limbs
Of boys. But the moment, clouding over,
Becomes again only an endless slipping of water

Over the spillways, and falls roaring in the ears
Until they ring, and the throat swollen
With failure and desire mingling there.

I could taste it in my mouth for days. It tasted

Like the wafer a friend said the Holy Ghost
Came wrapped up in. The Holy Ghost tastes like dust.
It liberates the body from the body so riddled

With rifle holes you can look right through us.
Look through us to what? To slums and shopping malls?
To one suburb joining another? Who grieves

On minimum wages? Look through us to that place—
Within sight of the trailer park and the truck stop—
Where Gettysburg could not be reenacted,

Where what was left of us on either side
Lay down our rifles, wept, embraced each other once.
That dust you taste in the Holy Ghost is us,

Dust ground into the windows you gaze out of,
And whether those windows burn or whether lights
Come on again in rows of quiet houses is a matter

Of how you treat him, sitting over there and still
Bleeding from a bad haircut, that captured soldier, that
Enemy, that risen dust, that boy, that stranger, you.

MAKE A LAW SO THAT THE SPINE REMEMBERS WINGS

So that the truant boy may go steady with the State,
So that in his spine a memory of wings
Will make his shoulders tense & bend
Like a thing already flown
When the bracelets of another school of love
Are fastened to his wrists,
Make a law that doesn't have to wait
Long until someone comes along to break it.

So that in jail he will have the time to read
How the king was beheaded & the hawk that rode
The king's wrist died of a common cold,
And learn that chivalry persists,
And what first felt like an insult to the flesh
Was the blank "o" of love.
Put the fun back into punishment.
Make a law that loves the one who breaks it.

So that no empty court will make a judge recall
Ice fishing on some overcast bay,
Shivering in the cold beside his father, it ought
To be an interesting law,
The kind of thing that no one can obey,
A law that whispers "Break me."
Let the crows roost & caw.
A good judge is an example to us all.

So that the patrolman can still whistle
"The Yellow Rose of Texas" through his teeth
And even show some faint gesture of respect
While he cuffs the suspect,
Not ungently, & says things like *OK,*

That's it, relax,
It'll go better for you if you don't resist,
Lean back just a little, against me.

IN THEORY

Before all the trees became bibles,
The forests & fields were pure,
The river sometimes forgot
That it was only a river,
And the tiger sometimes felt
It stood for more than itself,
More than the zoo all around it,
And the stone wished to be more
Than another stone among stones
In a building no longer there,
In a building made of stones.

In the bomb-magnified quiet,
Their flesh spilled out of their gowns,
It hung straight down from the windows
As we passed in the streets below,
And maybe one or two of them seemed
To be calling out to someone,
Calling, but without sound.
Later they said that, in theory,
The name of the town didn't matter.
It was all places, & none.
They said only theory was pure.
"And even then, only in theory,"
Is what I almost answered,
But it sounded better unsaid.

For though it was years later,
The breastbone & breasts of a girl
Who'd been dead less than an hour,
Still whitened over my head,
Was it her sun-dappled breasts that now

Seemed to turn all flesh into theory?
For only she could have known,
With all the other dead, whether
The place where it happened mattered.

They said we'd liberated them.
The trees & the streets were quiet,
And the stone was still a stone,
In a building made of stones,
In a building no longer there.
And the tiger was still a tiger,
A tiger that no one saw,
And the river ran silently on.

THE SPACE

The truth is, the whispered shape of his death
    Is too loud to hear.
It's in the sound of traffic overhead,
    Like a saw mill's whir
The moment after the lumber passes through it,
    Changes into time, into
Charred houses where the linen was stripped
    From beds & lace from
Dresses to bandage time together & hold it still
    For one more moment.
It began as no more than a joke with one wing
    That flew in circles
Through the smoke & talk of infinity assembled
    In Bell's Tavern.
Look around. There's nothing left of it.
    The wind leans
Against the girders, flange after gray-green flange
    That frames what's left,
A hush of space beneath a freeway overpass,
    Singed air & asphalt where
You can trace a pattern in the shattered glass
    Of a green bottle
Or read a destiny in spit before it dries,
    Or bear witness
To a drunk guy lurching to a stop
    As if to confer
With a god who swirls around him in a windblown
    Gust of trash,
Slow waltz of grit when the body isn't there,
    Flesh becoming pine
And a water that tastes like leather. Who
    Would ever have thought

The body could be poured? Like anything else?
        Who would have supposed
The body pouring out of the body in the stench
        Of resurrection?
One whiff of it & you wouldn't be able ever again
        To live with yourself.
You'd live with it as though it were someone else.
        A woman I once knew
Asked a gravedigger about exhuming remains, moving
        The dead from one place
To another. The gravedigger was neither old nor
        Young. He'd just been out
Of work too long. It was the only job he could get,
        He said. He had intended
To move on after a few months, but then. . . . He was
        Drinking a Coke, & resting.
"What's in the coffins," she asked him, "when, you know . . .
        You open them up?"
He looked at her briefly, "Just hair," he answered,
        "Just miles & miles of hair."
If the soul is just the story that it tells, then
        Did his answer, his smile,
The way he took his comb out of his back pocket
        And slicked his hair back,
Spite the soul with something like the soul?
        And who really gives a shit?
Except those who, like children who hope the story
        Never ends, & gather
To watch a fermented body pouring from a chalice,
        Or the boy who wished

To stay awake forever, & who, with matches & a spoon,
        After a while found a way
To do just that. They found him, face white & thin,
        Almost, as a communion host,
Dead in a little swanboat in the park, one foot dangling
        In the water of the pond.
My account of him is not a cautionary tale. As far
        As I'm concerned, he made it.
I could *feel* Death in that space where Booth, who was,
        As far as anyone can tell,
A space himself, or avenging angel, or absence, planned
        The assassination with two friends.
And so what if I could? The drunk was talking soundlessly
        And the traffic went on
Overhead. I rubbed my hand across my eyes as if
        To free them from what
Fettered them like a hawk's in a king's hand
        And when I opened them
A second later, the drunk was gone. The king was dead.
        I could see the nothing in
The space it ruled. Beside it there a small plaque
        Almost illegible, commemorating
The wrong thing, the recruitment of soldiers, sailors,
        Shiftless drunks, debtors,
Guys out of work, who fought the War of 1812, & then
        The Mexican War, & then . . .
But after that, the meadows turned to blood. What
        Happened after that was genocide.

The Self sounds like a guy raking leaves
Off his walk. It sounds like the scrape of the rake.
The soul is just a story the scraping tells.
The Self has no story. It is a sound. It scrapes
Against all things. He lets the rake do all
The talking now, the raked walk keeps the stars
From blowing out in the night sky
Above his house. It isn't music that he hears:
The sore screech of the wheel in the addict's voice,
Who, having kicked it, becomes the quiet shape
The shadow of his body makes. A rhythm
Only, 2/4 time, without a melody, the flesh
A lighter gray around the scar the stitches left.
Sore screech of the wheel that never rests,
Thin girl at her loom. Thin girl at her loom.

IDLE COMPANION

for Eric Walker & Abby Wolf

I thought I caught
A glimpse of it once
In a woman's nakedness,
Her shoulders in sunlight.
What was it that seemed
To gaze back at me,
And then was not there?

And didn't I hear it?
Wasn't that one scream
A complete stranger's cry,
Different from all the others
In the wailing of a madhouse?
It was. And then it wasn't.
But the wailing continued.
And soon it was impossible
To pick out that one
Cry from any other.

My hard-headed brunette
Pulls on a sweater,
And the roads are covered in mist.
And really the asylum
Was more often quiet
Than not. Even their wailing,
After a little while,
Was really a quiet in which
I could hear a janitor work
At a scuff mark on the floor.
And a nakedness that seemed

Familiar, then was not?
And some loony's aria
Drowned out by the whisper
Of steel wool on tiles?
Everything became different
By staying just the same.

My life has no witness
When I whisper to myself
"No, nothing there,"
Casting the flashlight over
The black drift of trees,
And the blacker, drifting sky,
And it's no good saying
That whoever it was
Is now only the nothing
The screen door cries out once
Behind me as it closes,
And then is quiet again,
The nothing that must dwell,
So idly, in its shriek.

And the tear in the screen
I never repaired,
And a run in her stockings
I noticed, once, in winter,
And the wake of a boat
Slowly closing over itself
And spreading, spreading
Into pines & silence.

Each thing's like another,
But not like it enough:
The shriek of the screen door
Unwilling to become
Either the madhouse wailing
Or the madhouse quiet
In the morning just after.
And the light still falling
Onto her shoulders in that
Moment when already
I was turning away,
Distracted by what
I cannot even remember,
A light seen just once,
Though it must have been
Flooding each object
In that room—keys,
Some change & our clothes
Strewn where we had
Left them the night before,
And two movie tickets,
Torn in half as usual,
That grow stranger & stranger
In the picture I have of them—
Two bits of paper
In a pale, & then even
A paler shade of green
Tossed onto a black sill
So many years ago—
That in this moment I find
Myself unwilling to do
Anything but gaze at them there—

Idle companion who stares
Into shop windows late,
Shuffler through rain & leaves,
And present though no one calls,
Are you what's twisted beneath
That lame girl on the porch,
Who reads beside the faint hymn
Of seven flies clustering
Over her bowl of overcast
Soup gone cold by now?
Or are you the sunlight on all
The roads when no one's there?
Or are you both, & neither one?
Unshakable companion,
The one friend left within
When all the others go,
And the only one I know
To be *criminally* sane,
Soul, what is your name?

ELEGY FOR THE INFINITE WRAPPED IN TINFOIL

His face itself a motionless white flame—
Serene three days now in the rear window of a bus
And still wide awake from half a gram of crystal—
The boy who set his girlfriend's house on fire
Said later in a threadbare accent with the sound
Of wind & the scrape of rusting metal in it
To the cop in Wheeling, "Didn't burn no *nothin'*,
I jus' walked a spell." In truth he felt he glided
There alone past eaves & lawns that flowed
Beside him then as if he'd loosened them
From every mooring but brimming moonlight
And the scent of ashes, a male smell overwhelming
All other blossoming of rose that wasn't his.
The mute porches & the dimming fireflies
Trapped in a bottle on a sill were things
He would not need in Florida . . .
And the syllables of *Florida* were like a fire.
Like the flicking of a girl's tongue inside his ear,
And they sounded like a fire when it caught
Its breath from shingles soaked in kerosene,
Like the flames' long kiss on door & windowframe
That grew the flame & the hunger of the flame . . .
He listens to the rain's staccato ceasing
On the tin roofs of the prison farm. He likes
Fire. He likes to think of fire. It is pure,
He thinks, & innocent, & it is like him
In the implacable fluent rising of its body,
Today, he is a flame. Yesterday,
He was also a flame, & the day before.
And the day before & the day before that.

III

A HOTEL ON FIRE

THE NECESSARY ANGEL

1.

Buddy you got no idea how fast it happens,
The tail gunner said to no one in particular,
And flicked the gunsight up with his index finger.
A moment later he turned to a wet rose
Blossoming all at once & too large
For the glassed-in hothouse turret to explain—
The bombardier still telling him a joke
Over the now quiet, frozen intercom.
The next day they fired on & sank
A harmless fishing junk with bleaching sails.
The one flag still believed in after the war,
Unfurling a lasting insult to a neighbor,
Was the index finger. Who christened it? When?
Half my country still believed in witches
The day they tricked the atom with a mirror.
And the sad whorl of flesh above the knuckle
Looks back at me as if to say the body
Is another's body, & the dark's *within* the dark.

2.

So the girl who received a whipping with a birch cane
In the schoolroom in front of all the others there,
Who witnessed in the passing weeks the bruises
Turn yellow & rose, until her flesh resembled
The random patterns blooming on late peaches—
Peaches & Cream is what the others called her,
Taunting her—is now a woman who watches, dry-eyed,
Above the cramped kitchen sink of a house trailer,
The way the wind whips the weeds in a vacant lot,
The way it blows trash against the chain-link fence
Along the interstate. She is just watching it get darker,

The dark seeming to spill out of the dark, out of what
Is already dark. She moves her hips forward until
They touch the sink, withdraws them slowly, pushes them
Close again. *Some enchanted fuckin' evening,* she says,
A moment or two later. She sticks her tongue out
At the dark. She begins chopping things up for a salad.
Buddy you got no idea how dark it is, the blood swears
Against the glass. She hears the light hissing above her
In the kitchen, & thinks she may well be the witch
They said she was. A power without a switch to turn
It on. The birch cane falling through the autumn light
Of the classroom, the switch that left her in the dark.
The switch that can't explain her life, or why she's poor
And white in all this dark. It's 1952.
White Trash—that's what all her neighbors call her.
White Trash—the sprawl of a wave on a rock is all
That's left within the words when I say them slowly now.
She isn't in them anymore. And whenever she appears
It's 1952 & she is making dinner.
This is before the country enters history. This is before
The president is fast-forwarded out of his own blood—
Lifted & dropped like a sheet of paper in the wind—
Into the front seat of the white limousine. Wide awake.
If you still the frame the president looks wide awake.
Like the woman in the kitchen of her trailer making
Salad, her script for Benzedrine refilled, the bottle of it
On the counter there. Wide awake in 1952,
And as the dark filled the field outside she'd masturbate
With a cucumber, then slice it up & serve it to
Her husband in his salad. She'd watch him douse it
In Thousand Island dressing & wash it down with bourbon
While she smoked—she wasn't hungry—across from him

At the table. It was the moment of the day
She waited for, the wind hissing outside the trailer,
Her husband still in uniform. Then she would switch
The cigarette to her left hand, reach between her thighs
With her right, & slowly unfurl her index finger.
It stood right up to him in the wordless dark beneath
The table. Death & Resurrection & the dark we are.

    3.

And against the dark? The lobby's polished brass,
The bright light of a hotel barber shop, & a music
In a chair, his mind on nothing. Beyond the window,
Is Hartford in a downpour & a fallen world where,
Every Tuesday afternoon for twelve years,
My hill witch does Wallace Stevens' nails while he reads
The New York Times. Sometimes it's Bergson or
Santayana, the book folded into the newspaper so it looks
As if he's reading the paper, & sometimes it's the paper,
And at least twice each time he visits Stevens
Finds himself staring at her breasts
That rise & fall to the quickened rhythm of her breath.
He feels her warm breath on his fingernails
As she polishes them. He watches her & he thinks
Of the clouds slowly changing shape in the night sky
Of Florida, & knows if he reaches out, & touches her,
Touches the swelling cotton fabric of her sweater,
He will begin the long fall that culminates
In a commonplace of wave sprawl & a coastline
Filling with service stations, taco stands, motels,
A screen door banging endlessly in the wind.
And Oh he wants to! The desire has less to do with her
Than with a wish to fall & keep falling silently.

Out of the world. All it requires is this slight gesture,
His index finger uncurling like a thought
Made flesh to taste the withering cold to come.
She could feel him watching her.
And said to herself, as she dusted his nails & blew
Hot little breaths on each one of them,
"So you wanna floor show with your manicure."
The next time she undid a button on her blouse,
Stopped filing for a second, & looked into his eyes . . .
He couldn't work for a week. He waited for a warm,
Overcast afternoon in March before he tried to touch her,
And waited for his body to open like a parachute.
She was buffing the pink fingernails
Of his right hand when he discovered that his left
Index finger would not move. He tried again, & found
He could not move any muscle. He stared
At the swimming print of the paper on his lap
And saw instead the wave sprawl on the rock
And the beach growing colder, emptier than
The sound it held. Then he was falling toward it
In the dark. "It's all right, it'll be all right," he heard
A voice saying. It was like the voice of a mother
In the night, the calm in its wake a widening, spiraling
Calm, like the pattern in a carpet he remembered,
Like a voice from childhood whispering in his ear,
The calm voice of a woman in a quiet house,
A voice he knew, a voice he had always known.
It was embarrassing to wake & find it *was*
The voice of a woman whispering in his ear,
To find he'd fainted in the shop while she
Was giving him a manicure, & to find her touch
On his face was gentler than the remembered

Touch of his wife, or mother, or any other touch,
That it was like the night air of Florida, incorporeal,
The finally dissolving pattern of a final heaven.

    4.

After that, the men who fell & were found frozen
In ditches, their parachutes spreading around them
Like picnic blankets, were much like the men he saw
Strolling behind lawnmowers in the summer dark.
Lights came on in houses & the stars came out.
All of it seemed a part of what was uneventful,
A part of all there was that went on falling
Into a silence that seemed to enter everything
Or else had been there all along without their knowing.
They felt its presence in the gauzy, late afternoon
Light falling through the windows of the lobby. As he
Read the paper, as she went on filing his nails—
The silence of the empty barber's chair next to them,
The silence of jars on a shelf & magazines in a rack—
Was neither the clothing of things nor the nakedness
Of things. It wasn't this. It wasn't that. It was
The blank, the *the* that set the whole a-spin.
He would begin to doze off, his hand in hers,
And the sound of the nail file was the sound of his steps
Racing over the dry beach grass on a winter day
As if he were still a boy one step ahead of the quiet . . .
But where the quiet overtakes him everything
Is changed: her breasts awaken to his touch
Only to disappear into this cold air in his palms.
And if streams unthaw, if the lazy gauze
Of vegetation comes back along the street, it finds
She isn't there, that she is air & fire & absence.

The file sounds like the gate scraping shut behind him.
And the world tinged in frost. It glitters in the sun.
He is surprised to find he's already walking past
What has become the illegible. In its raw light,
Where the eyes of the poor are like flaking paint,
Where an expressionless boy with a headband leans
On the crumpled fender of a car, & spits once
As he passes, there is no other sign—only the marquee,
Flashing, half-lit, on the motel beneath the overpass.
In the room the headboard of the bed shakes
From the ceaseless traffic passing overhead,
His things in a little jar in the bathroom tremble
And tinkle constantly. He does not understand why,
When he reaches out to test how firm the peaches are,
The store clerk in a white apron threatens him
With a baseball bat. And all of it happens in silence.
The color of the apron seems to change each time
The clerk raises the bat in both hands, changes
Like a remembered beach that was now in sunlight,
Now in the shadow of clouds—all there is left
Of the picked-over, looted, empty attic of heaven.
What was the worm doing there, at heaven's gate?
But now it had eaten Heaven, now the light along
The coast was real, & was light. Now there was nothing,
Nothing but the empty, stretching arm of the beach
Beneath the empty clouds. It was up to him to put it
Back together, & he thought he might begin now
With the wave sprawl on the rock & the tern's cry.
Outside, the scent of exhaust, the smell of baking
Bread, seemed more familiar now than the smell
Of sex, that sudden garlic overwhelming the dry
Lilac that had become the body of his wife.

The hymen of his soul parted as he walked
For traffic, for the rain changing back again to snow.
And the home he enters is not his home although
A doily on a sofa seems the perfect expression
Of a perfect quiet except . . . it isn't there. He'd taken
Those exuberant, tasteless fantails of a distant aunt
And thrown them in the trash bin years ago . . .
He looks again & hears her saying, "It'll be all right,"
He sees that the doily isn't there, sees that the only
Embroidery is invisible, is what the quiet
Is making within the stillness of the study.
He hears his wife's step, then the creak of her chair
Above him. She is reading there in her room or sewing
Something. She is there. And she is not there.
He closes his eyes a moment & sees a rock,
And then the sprawl of a wave against the rock,
And then the gleaming rock again, & he feels afraid.
Had the woman creaking in the chair above him
Become a rock & the sprawl of a wave against
The rock? Had she become the terns' cries
As they gathered once, just once, into a tight,
Converging knot above the surf that just
As suddenly undid itself, & was not, was gone
Like the drying froth the wave left as it receded,
Like the windblown sparks of a fire on a beach
That left him walking there alone in winter?
He hears the creaking of her chair on the floor above—
What will he say of them? Her step, the creaking
Of her chair is asking, asking, asking: it is defiant.
He bends his head a little as if he is listening
To the wood grain in his desk turn into music.
But the grain in the wood is silent & the boy is dead.

And the sad whorls of flesh, or wood swirl of the knuckle
Above the forefinger, thumb, & middle finger that hold on
Tight to the pen, Swan or Waterman, for the carnival ride,
Hesitate a second at the top of the rickety scaffold—
At the top of the Wild Worm he can smell the sea—
Before the steep drop, the rush through the summer air,
On which is written, "It is an illusion that we ever lived."
It is what the wave sprawl on the rock said & the boy
Who was dead. What is not written anywhere is what
Was said in the moment after—said finally & once
To the bare breasts of the woman kneeling there,
To the manicurist herself chewing gum on the bus
As she goes home to her small apartment, living alone,
The lights of the city glittering in the snowy air;
Said so that it can never be unsaid, by the creaking
Of his wife's chair, by the ironic scraping of limbs
Against a wall, until the two sounds are all there is—
Filling the house with their brief & thoughtless triumph.

POEM ENDING WITH A HOTEL ON FIRE

Poor means knowing the trees couldn't care less

Whether you carve the initials of your enemies
All over the trunk's white bark,

Or whether this sleep beneath them is your last.

In the contorted figures meant to represent their sleep,
The statistics never show the deep shade in the park,

The mother appearing in the dark of someone within whose
Sprawled arms clear gin & black tar mingle
To compose the blood's unwritable psalm.

The blackening church bells say the poor are wrong,
So does the traffic stalling on the bridge; so does the lazy swirl
Of current underneath it all, a smile fading in the dark.

What I love is the way you would whisper against
The current, into the dark,

"But what you mean by *poor* is . . . some figure & concealment
By which they are forgotten. But the figure itself is a kind

Of poverty. I don't mean just . . . money. I mean poverty

In the widest possible . . . *sense.*" There was the sound

Of crickets in a ravine I listened to so closely one evening

It became only a vast chirring, then a thing not there, then

The roar of a fire. It was like being, or pretending to be,

Without speech. To be without speech means no one
Listening, & that the flames scaling the neighborhood like mirrors

Cannot even pretend to. This is

Where the poor are not permitted to see themselves,

This is why money mirrors nothing so accurately it tempts us

To seek our reflections in the passing, leafy idyll

Of a water so toxic by now it would scald you if it were
Real—for what is engraved upon it still represents

A wilderness—or a flash of a green silence almost alive
In the palm of your hand—that stands for one. And what

Secessionist keeps whispering in your ear? And whose
Eye, removed from a human face, stares from a pyramid

Like a bicep's inscrutable tattoo? And what mansion floats
in its mosses & a landscaping so thick you cannot pick out

The slave, snoring or dead, or holding a towel to his head

Where an ear had been, in the shade of the willow there?

Once in a hotel in Cincinnati, I saw a woman decorated,

Like a kind of human Christmas tree, in money. All down
the buttons of her blouse & in fact all over her blouse & skirt,

The men, for whom, I heard later, she had been hired as
A private dancer, had pinned twenties, hundreds, fifties,

Rolls of smaller bills—& as the alarm blared its one note &

The beige smoke—billowy, calm signature of whoever had set
The upper floors on fire—began filling

The corridor, we arrived at the elevator in the same
Moment, & waited—I in shorts & a faded T-shirt with three

Naked Jamaicans on it who were, once, The Itals,
And she in the most expensive dress I had ever seen—

And when the elevator didn't show we ran down the steel & concrete
Stairs that seemed to ring & ring with our steps.

Later, in the lobby bar, her purse so stuffed with bills
The bartender simply said, "It's cool," & raised both hands

Above his head when we tried to pay, she would talk only
Of her one obsession, which had nothing to do with money nor

Swaying to music, nor men,

But with purebred Abyssinian cats, the trouble she went to,

Taking them—traveling with four howling cages behind her
In the back of a station wagon—to shows all over

The Midwest. The worst part though, she said, was that
The shows were rigged, the judges were paid off—

So every winner—she had exhaustively researched all this,
She told me—every winner descended from families that had arrived

On the *Mayflower,* & did I know

Most of America was in the control of people who spent whole
Afternoons "daydreaming, running combs through these Siamese

And long-haired Persians fat as sofa pillows?" "No kidding,"
I said. And did I read about how they'd tried

To frame her in Chicago . . . ? "Do I look capable of Murder One?"
She turned to me, the glint in her eye revealing nothing.

"No," I said, "But what about Murder Two? Isn't that just . . .
The same thing done with a lot more feeling?"

In her laughter you could hear leaves scraping the cold streets.
If you listened for it. If you listened hard enough.

⸺

The fire in the hotel had begun as nothing more
Than the prank of a child who'd gotten high, after school,

By inhaling gasoline fumes in a vacant lot, & who then rode,
With a gas can carried in a paper bag, the elevator to

The Starlight Terrace restaurant where he looked beyond
Frayed tablecloths & over the entire city before a waiter

Picked him up by his long hair & shoved him into an open

Elevator in which falling solitude the boy
Splashed gasoline all over the fake wood paneling & plaid

Carpet, stepped out of it two floors later, & then, with that
Quick & graceful turning gesture from which the body makes

The thoughtless beauty of a hook shot from mid-court, tossed
A match inside before the door could close. And though it took

The fire crew less than an hour to clear two floors & put the last
Sparks out, I kept thinking of the elevator descending to some

Small family probably in from the sticks, probably on their way to visit
A dying aunt or sister, who, after blowing all their savings to stay

In a room decorated with the overcast melancholy of a cheap
Utrillo print, waited there in the fatigued aftertaste

Failure left them with, as if to think it over, in that moment

When the doors opened onto flames.

In the photographs she showed me the Abyssinians looked

Emaciated, &, though I couldn't say why, like a species that
Had survived its own extinction. Their pale eyes suggested

Nothing at all. They looked back like the face of famine,

Their thin, ridged spines older than even the ancient
Illustrations of cats on tombs, cats that had been the pets

Of kings & now slept beside them in the straitjacketed,
Dry, whirlpool of bandages they had wrapped kings in so that

They might descend without distractions. Did the doors
Of tombs open onto flames? The faces of the cats

Caught in the photographs would never tell.

Their gray fur was like blurred print or the blank, chirring
Blizzard on the TV set above the bar. Nothing would tell.

Once in a blizzard in a foreign city, having lost my way,
I wondered what it would be like to be one of those—blind
Drunk, high, or homeless—who would have no alternative except

To freeze to death, & thought how, after the initiation of pain,
They say it is like being lulled to sleep, the way the snow

Appears to faint as it swirls in the locked doorways of shops,
The way this would be the last thing that appeared to you

There, before whatever was left of you became gradually
Confused with a small part of the upsway

Of snow & wind.

It is all a matter of confusing yourself with something else:

The soul curls up in a doorway, & lets the snow swirl around it.

And . . . not just money then, but . . . *poverty,* I thought, in the widest
Possible . . . *sense* of the term, would

Be. . . . But then I knew what it would be.

For a moment I could hear the cats howling in their steel cages,
Their thin spines turning in circles.

Tattoo on a forearm & shriek of the wind, & no figure drawn
In the night's silent contemplation by which

The poor might be forgotten;

And not you beside me in the dark but only a dry fern & a bible
In the room, the rain beginning its long descent onto the roof—

Its sound the chirring of crickets in a ravine.

I could almost hear . . . no, I could only imagine hearing it. And that

Is what it has become:

Having to imagine, having to imagine everything,

In detail, & without end.

IV

THE CONDITION OF PITY IN OUR TIME

ELEGY WITH A DARKENING TRAPEZE INSIDE IT

The idea turned out to be no more than a cart wheel
Stuck in mud, & unturned fields spreading to the horizon while
Two guys in a tavern went on drinking *tsuica* & recalling their one

Accomplishment in life—the seduction of a virgin on the blank
Pedestal of a statue where Stalin had once stood.

The State is an old man's withered arm.

The only surviving son of Jesus Christ was Karl Marx.
You can tell by the last letter of his name,
Which has the shape & frail balance of an overturned cross

On a windswept hillside. It marked the end of things.
Of lumber that rots & falls. The czar is a shattered teacup,

The trouble with a good idea is that it has to work:

The only surviving son of Jesus Christ survives now
Mostly in English departments & untended graves.

One thing he said I still remember, a thing that's never there
When I try to look it up, was: "Sex should be no more important . . .
Than a glass of water." It sounded vaguely like the kind of thing

Christ might have said if Christ had a sense of humor.
The empty bar that someone was supposed to swing to him
Did not arrive, & so his outstretched flesh itself became

A darkening trapeze. The two other acrobats were thieves.

My colleague Otto Fick, who twenty years ago
Wrote brilliant lectures on the air, sometimes
Would pause & seem to consult notes left
On a podium, & then resume. A student once
Went up after class to look at them & found
Only a blank sheet of paper. Nothing there.
"In theory, I believe in Marx. In fact, my wife
Has to go in next week for another
Biopsy. Fact is disbelief. One day it swells up
In front of you, the sky, the sunlight on everything,

Traffic, kids on surfboards waiting for the next
Big set off San Onofre. It's all still there . . . just
There for someone else, not for you." This is what
My friend Otto told me as we drove to work.

I worked with men in vineyards once who were paid
In wages thin as water, cash that evaporated & rose like heat.
They lived in rows of makeshift sheds the owner hauled

Into an orchard too old to bother picking anymore,
And where, at dusk, a visible rushing hunger

Raced along the limbs of the trees surrounding them.
Their kids would watch it happen until a whole tree would seem
To vanish under it. There were so many of them.

By then the rats were flying over a sickening trapeze of leaves
And the tree would darken suddenly. It would look like brown water

Rushing silently & spreading everywhere

Before it got dark anyway & the kids went in.
"There was more rats in there than there was beads on all the rosaries of the dead.
We wen' to confession all the time then 'cause we thought we might disappear

Under them trees. There was a bruja in the camp but we dint go to her no more.
She couldn't predict nothing. And she'd always cry when you asked her questions,"

A woman said who had stayed there for a while.

Every revolution ends, or it begins, in memory:
Someone remembering her diminishment & pain, the way
Her scuffed shoes looked in the pale light,
How she inhaled steel filings in the grinding shed
For thirty years without complaining once about it,
How she might have done things differently. But didn't.
How it is too late to change things now. How it isn't.

COL TEMPO

The body is not above mockery:
Even one who has failed grows hungry.
The woman in the painting's blind & wears
A sign around her neck. You never entirely forget
The gray sheen, like steel, of the cataract
Covering the one eye that remains open.
When I say *you* to what isn't there I mean *me*.
It is as if our language did this to us,
As if, at some point, we became others in it,
Others in a crowd of others who were just like us,
Who strolled through the *Accademia* in Venice,
Where sometimes it was raining & sometimes it wasn't.
We stared at the blind woman with the sign
Around her neck, & knew we had failed in everything.
Donatello is dead leaves & you can't
Feel sorry for him without pretending to.
You might be able to feel sorry for pretending
To feel sorry, especially if you are a child, but . . .
That was the lesson in the painting,
Which was by Donatello once & then by Giorgione.
There's not much point in confessing to things
These days. Still, I love the sound of gunfire
In my neighborhood, always slightly distant,
At least three blocks away on most nights.
Something in me loves the slightly distant
Sound of gunfire, & something else does not,
Because it thinks it shouldn't. It must be that
Failure enlarges you & divides you, like a cell.
The two of them are resting their hands on the table
After writing this. Writing this because
we can't afford to travel anywhere.
The summer's spiderwebs glisten in the eaves

Beyond the window. It's not as if we're poor,
Or anything. It's not like we're sitting here complaining
About it, about sitting here, I mean.
It's what we've been longing to do all along. In a way,
You could say we're celebrating something,
Even if it doesn't have a name.
It seems so limitless, the litter in the streets,
The large families of the poor, the stars over it all.

IF HE CAME & DIMINISHED ME & MAPPED MY WAY

Who was there in the uncountable stars, in the distance,
And in the cold glittering?
Who leaned with the wind against the trees all day,

And who slept in the swing's empty stillness under them?

Who was present in the pattern of the snake fading
Into the pattern of the leaves again?

And who presided over the empty clarity of water falling,
Water spreading into a thin, white veil
Glimpsed just once in a moment clear & empty as a heaven—

Once heaven has been swept clean of any meaning?

Whose childhood is no more than a blackened rafter,
Something left after fire has swept through it?

It is years later when I come back to that place where I'd hiked once,
And somehow lost the trail, & then,
For a while, walked in the Company of Hallucination & Terror,

And noted afterward, like something closing within me,

That slight disappointment when I found

The trail again, when the rocks & trees took
Their places beside it, & I went on, up
To the summit of bare rock & the smoke rising

Lazily out of the small hut there, soup & coffee,
A table of brochures & maps of hiking trails

I browsed through idly, recalling being lost,
Recalling the way each rock looked, how
Expressionless it was, how each

Was the same as another, without a face, until
I understood I was completely lost, & then

How someone so thin I could have passed my hand through him
Walked beside me there, & though I did not dare look
To see who it was, I glanced sideways once to see

How his ribs depicted famine, & how his steps beside me

Were effortless, were like air gliding through air
Again & again without haste or hesitation

As the trail appeared again under my feet & rose
Upward in a long series of switchbacks

Through a forest I no longer believed in.

What I felt was diminishment, embarrassment, &

He must be starving by now, his face multiplying
To become the haunted faces of others in the streets,

Where to walk at night is to be flayed alive beneath

The freezing rain, where the trees glisten with ice,
And the lights are left on all night in the big stores,

If the pleasure of his company does not last,
If the terror of his company does not last,
If forgetting or remembering him are the same, now,

As I slow the car, pull over to the curb,
And wait until I see my dealer emerge
Cautiously as always from the fenced walkway beside

An abandoned house in a street of abandoned,
Or nearly vacant & for sale, houses,

And if, by getting high, one can live
Effortlessly anywhere for a little while, if

Me & my dealer, a Jamaican named John Donne,

Gaze out at the rain & listen to the hushed clatter
Of an empty metal shopping cart someone pushes through the rain,

If we gaze out at the living, & at the dead, & they are the same,
If the sound of a bus going past & the sound of the wind
Are the same, are what is left to listen to in the world,

Though the world sleeps, & the trees above us sleep, their limbs
Mending themselves in the cold wind,

Then both of Us would avert our Faces from His Face.

FRANÇOIS VILLON ON THE CONDITION OF PITY IN OUR TIME

Frères humains, qui après nous vivez,
Soon they'll have the speed freak twisting
On a scaffold, soon the birds
Will come to peck out his eyes, & when
He's too weak & exhausted to turn
His head away, they'll do it, too,
They'll peck his eyes right out.
You'll want to watch it happen, you'll want
To witness it. You'll want to see Paolo
And Francesca almost touch before
They're swept away again, him in one line
Waiting for rations, her in another one,
Both of them naked, standing there,
Cock & nipples shriveled in the cold.

Frères humains, qui après nous vivez,
N'ayez les cœurs contre nous endurcis.
In wind & rain, the lovers almost touch,
and gulls & ravens settle on his shoulders.
You watch because you love to watch.
In plague times, the streets fill with *voyeurs.*
I know. The sockets of my eyes are dry
As little thimbles made of blistered skin,
And that inward savor of the infinite
Is salt again, one wave hidden in another.
We're broken buttons, we're blown dust.
There's not one tear left in all of us.
I know, for I am François Villon, murderer,
Thief: pustules, blisters, triumphing sores,
Your disappearing likeness on the cross!

ANONYMOUS SOURCE

Hoping to escape, I frequented the docks & went unseen,
Ignoring the cold & a colder sea in which there was, at least, no change of regime.
And later, in a tour bus requisitioned by the police,
I gazed out at the examples of closed casinos lining the beach,
Seaweed wreathing the busy, baroque stillness of their verandas.
As if we needed such reminders.
The voices over the loudspeakers, galvanized & trite,
Were loud enough to keep everything quiet.
And just as one of the symptoms of schizophrenia is a constant & inappropriate
    inclination toward spontaneous & delayed rhyming,
I was, I think, betrayed by bad timing.
Refinement? Good taste?
I've found, at least in revolutions, that they simply have no place.
In fact, a few weeks after the coup even the pettiest
Of newly appointed public officials was able to furnish his office
With a choice of elaborate heirlooms
Confiscated from some country estate: cloisonné vases became spittoons;
Pets ate from dishes of silver & cut glass;
And peasants slept on ottomans & love seats displaying some outlandish
Pattern of swans violently intertwined with last century's roses.
Below, in the plaza, I watched as those charged with treason were sprayed with firehoses,
Then made to stand at attention all day in handcuffs & a lukewarm rain.
Behind them, the wild blossoming of cherries looked insane.
I watched them because . . . there wasn't much else to do,
Having been made to wait for an interview.
I can't say I felt much nostalgia for the king & queen,
So enchanted by their own story
They ended stripped & hung on hooks like sides of beef, smoked & curing.
Mostly I missed the gambling.
Beyond that, the new methods of torture, intended, I suppose, to be ironic, remained
Altogether too tacitly the same—

The princess who was made to appear at a mock recital,

But missing her tongue now, & who afterward was forced to attend the reception
    wearing a tiny, hand-made bridle

And blinders over her face?

Thugs from the countryside, in uniforms now, & sniffing brandy & tulips, took turns
    holding the reins;

The answer to their prolonged parlor game

Was, of course,

An obvious pun, in English, on their word for horse.

So cruelty returned to its usual throne. And, in a few weeks,

The rebels who had come to power were sipping iced drinks

With the former administrators on the daffodil-laden, roof-top terrace

Of an empty hotel that was, once, the downtown winter palace.

But then, how could they do otherwise, once everyone was free?

Certainly they took no pleasure in the routine inspection of factories

And schools, nor in the feigned

Attention they paid to their president,

Still dressed in camouflaged fatigues, & yet so absent-

Minded, so paranoid, he forgot me entirely. Thank God (or something) for paranoia;

I was given a sinecure,

A tedious but mild post with the Department of Agriculture,

And a wheezing Renault with threadbare tires.

And as more & more farms went bankrupt with new policies, I looked away.

In the provinces, I sat in the stippled sunlight of the cafés,

And read the foreign papers,

Or, loitering, strolling through thatched villages, I began to admire

The precise & gradually fading patina on posters

That had once depicted, though too clearly for me, some pastoral scene

In which cattle moved lissomely as wheat,

And liberators waved from hillsides; it was all sweet, yes, & stupid,

Like life itself, or the end of *Candide.*

And in the city I gambled illegally in my forgotten neighborhood

Shaded by mulberries as still & untroubled as druids—

The same punks & pensioners below, the same pigeons above,
The street lined with billboards relentlessly displaying couples in love—
At first, of course, with their carbines, then later with an Idea, &, presumably, each other.
And the cafés filling with traffickers
In the Black Market items: Levi's, hashish, Black Sabbath T-shirts?
There are days when I love it here.
And although this country remains closed to visitors,
I, for one, am thankful. To the West, the gates at the border wear a covering
Of alternately bleached & frostbitten, unmolested & therefore unwithering
Vines that grow in an untalkative leisure, a sleeping platoon . . .
(It can look really unnerving under a full moon)
Of the rankest vegetation.
Obviously the guards in their tower above it have never felt the slightest inclination
To even try to hack through it.
And so it came to me as something of a surprise
That on the borders of the remotest provinces, & almost always in private,
Everyone has begun to whisper of the ruin
That must come to this country as inevitably as the first tourist,
And, in the rural currency of their dreams, they worship
Something overwhelming, a god in another style, one so aloof & uninformed,
So camouflaged as the tuneless
Snow, or shade, He resists even a prolonged examination,
And makes any escape from the eventual thrill of His contamination
Seem frankly impossible,
And, for the time being, not at all desirable.
Now that's *style.*
And these peasants won't negotiate their long sleep until
It has restored that sheep-tenanted, stone eyesore on the hill,
That castle whose attic is starlight & a heaven, vast, unfinished—
Each twilight like a blueprint in which something is always missing.
In fact, hiking toward that castle at dawn, each time, as I drew nearer, I've watched it
    gradually vanish!

There's nothing up there but goat trails leading nowhere, stunted pines, & mist.

If it *is* there, then I don't exist . . .

No. That's not it, either. I finally write all of this

In the suburban boudoir of the magistrate's lovely, rebellious, gum-chewing daughter

Asleep beside me. And as my pen hesitates one last time above this paper,

My hand, recollecting the strap

Tied over it, the rain falling outside the windows of the asylum

That held it captive

In the moment before the slightly rusted electrodes were fastened,

Even now it rejoices only in what it is.

And I find myself gazing at a wall recently remodeled

In a flocked chintz paper, its motionless but swelling pattern of enormous lilacs, as
     precise & repetitive as Hell's,

Recalls the first light entering the first garden,

A pattern as carnivorous as change—

As now, the antique sound of the spinning loom in the lane,

Slowing to a final stop, gives out a brief, sore squeal—

And writing it down, scoring the sound like a music until he is blent to the only miracle,

Even the one listener seems, brief as he is, unnecessarily real.

OCEAN PARK #17, 1968: HOMAGE TO DIEBENKORN

What I remember is a carhop on Pico hurrying
Toward a blue Chevy,

A crucifix dangling from its rearview mirror
That jiggled as the driver brushed

A revolver against it, in passing, before tucking it
Behind his back & beginning to joke with her.

What I remember
Is the smooth arc the gun made & the way

Jesus shimmied to the rhythm.

Someday I'll go back to the place depicted
By the painting, boarded over by the layers of paint

And abandoned,

And beneath the pastel yellows I'll find
The Bayside Motel & the little room

With the thin, rumpled coverlet,

And sit down, drinking nothing but the night air
By the window, & wait for her to finish

Dressing, one earring, then another,

And wait until the objects in the room take back
Their shapes in the dawn,

And wait until

Each rumpled crease in the sheets & pillowcase
Is as clear as a gift again, & wait—

At a certain moment, that room, then all the rooms
Of the empty Bayside,

Will turn completely into light.

I place a cup on the sill & listen for the faint
Tock of china on wood, & . . .

That moment of light is already this one—
Sweet, fickle, oblivious, & gone:

My hand hurrying across the page to get there
On time, that place

Of undoing—

Where the shriek of the carhop's laugh,
And the complete faith of the martyr, as he spins & shimmies in the light,

And the inextricable candor of doubt by which Diebenkorn,
One afternoon, made his presence known

In the yellow pastels, then wiped his knuckles with a rag—

    Are one—are the salt, the nowhere & the cold—

The entwined limbs of lovers & the cold wave's sprawl.

THRESHOLD OF THE OBLIVIOUS BLOSSOMING

When I said one blossom desires the air,
Another the shadows, I was free
Of desires. Beyond the doorsill the café tables

Were empty because it was raining.
The rain was empty as well, & there was no poignancy

Left in it when I looked up at it falling, & went on
Sitting inside & waiting for my dealer to show up so I could buy
Two grams of crystal methedrine from her, talk for a moment,

And finish my coffee.

When I thought of the petals of the magnolia blossom
Flattened by passing traffic to the pavement & the gradual
Discoloration of them, their white like that of communion dresses

Becoming gray & a darker gray moment by moment,
When I knew I wanted them to mean nothing

And suggest everything, desire rushed back into things,
But not into the blossoms & not into the air.

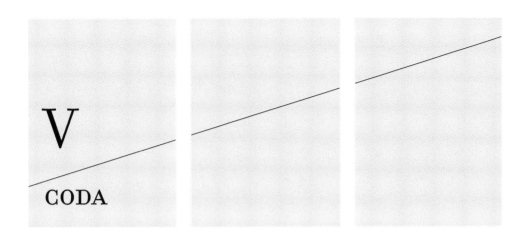

V

CODA

GOD IS ALWAYS SEVENTEEN

This is the last poem in the book. In a way, I don't even want
to finish it. I'd rather go to bed & jack off under the covers

But I'd probably lose interest in it & begin wondering about God,
And whether He's tried the methamphetamine I sent Him yet, & if He still

Listens to the Clash & whether the new job He got for Mozart
As a janitorial assistant in Tulsa is working out.

Besides, I can't imagine a body in the first faint stirrings of arousal
Without feeling sorry for it now, & anyway, I've built a fire in the fireplace

And I don't have a fire screen yet, & have to watch it until it goes out,
Even the last lukewarm ember. It isn't my house.

It belongs to a bank in St. Louis somewhere & they have four thousand
Different ways to punish me if the place goes up in flames, including the guys

From Medellín who work for them now & specialize in pain.
Besides, it's still winter everywhere & maybe you want to hear a story

With a fire burning quietly beside it. The story on this night when it
Got really cold, & the darkness of the night spreading

Over the sky seemed larger than it should have been, though
Nobody mentioned it. It was something

You didn't feel like bringing up if you were sitting in a bar
Among your friends. But all that happened was the night kept getting larger

Then larger still, & then there was a squeal of brakes
Outside the bar, & then what they call in prose the "sickening" crunch

Of metal as two cars collided & in a little while the guy went back to telling
This story in which the warm snow was falling on the yard

Where he & the other prisoners were exercising. I guess the guy
Had evidently done some time, though everyone listening was too polite

To bring it up. And what happened in it was a clerk bleeding to death
In a 7-Eleven, & the guy telling it called 911 for an ambulance, & the police found both

Cash from the till & the gun on him when they arrived. He didn't think he'd shot
Anyone that night or anyone ever & was surprised & puzzled

When they made a match on the gun, the clerk lived to testify, & they convicted
Him. No one along the bar said anything when he'd finished

Telling it, & the night went on enlarging in the story, & I think our silence
Cut him loose & let him go falling. And one by one, we paid & got up & left

And went out under the stars. I have a child who isn't doing well in school.
It's not his grades. It's that he can't wake up.

He misses his morning classes & doesn't answer when I call & doesn't
Return my calls. The last time I saw him we took the train down from Connecticut

To New York & wandered around Times Square. We went into this record store
And pretended to browse through some albums there

Because we didn't know what to say to each other. It was night. It was just
Before the Christmas season, & the clerks in the store

Would call out loudly Can I Help Anybody & Can I Help Someone & there was
Some music playing & something inconsolable

And no longer even bitter in the melody & I will never forget
Being there with him & hearing it & wondering what was going to become of us.

NOTES

The dates, where listed, represent those corresponding to the last saved drafts on Larry Levis's computer. In some cases, subsequent handwritten revisions on a hard-copy draft of a poem were also incorporated into a piece in an attempt to establish as near a "final" draft as possible.

"Gossip in the Village": This poem was originally titled "Fifth Season." It was written in Iowa City, in the spring of 1982, and its title was later changed to "Gossip in the Village." I first saw the poem as part of a manuscript titled *Adolescence,* an early draft of the collection that was to become Levis's fourth book, *Winter Stars.* At various times, the manuscript was also titled *Trouble;* in 1984, Levis told Bruce Boston he was thinking of calling his new book *Sensationalism.* After Boston discouraged him, Levis consulted with Philip Levine and published the book, in 1985, as *Winter Stars.*

"New Year's Eve at the Santa Fe Hotel, Fresno, California": This poem was written as a gift for Levis's close friends Bruce and Marsha Boston.

"*La Strada*": The movie by Fellini, from 1954, starring Anthony Quinn and Giulietta Masina. The final line of the poem appears also with a slight variation within the body of the poem, "Boy in Video Arcade," from Levis's posthumous collection, *Elegy.*

"Carte de l'Assassin à M. André Breton": The title refers to one of the Surrealist games popular with Breton and other poets and artists.

"The Worm in the Ear": Accepted for publication before Levis's death, this poem appeared posthumously in the *American Poetry Review.*

"Twelve Thirty One Nineteen Ninety Nine": This poem is dated 11-9-92.

"Ghazal": This poem also appears in the manuscript of poems titled *Adolescence.*

"Make a Law So That the Spine Remembers Wings": Dated 2-13-96.

"In Theory": Dated 2-25-95.

"Idle Companion": The poem is dedicated to Eric Walker and Abby Wolf, poets who attended the University of Iowa Writers' Workshop and were close friends of Levis and Marcia Southwick during the years they taught there.

"The Necessary Angel": This homage to Stevens is the most complete version existing in Levis's papers. See also his poem "Elegy with an Angel at Its Gate," section 3, titled "Stevens" (in *Elegy*).

"Poem Ending with a Hotel on Fire": See the Afterword.

"Elegy with a Darkening Trapeze inside It": The term *tsuica* refers to a Romanian plum brandy. The poem is dated 11-10-95.

"Col Tempo": Dated 8-3-95.

"If He Came & Dimished Me & Mapped My Way": Dated 5-22-95. See John Berryman's *The Dream Songs* (13) and John Donne's "Meditation XVII." The poem uses in its opening section mild variants of lines also found in the opening sections of "Ghost Confederacy," which is undated.

"François Villon on the Condition of Pity in Our Time": Dated 12-9-95. For my extended note on this poem, see "On 'François Villon on the Condition of Pity in Our Time' by Larry Levis" from the November 2014 issue of *Poetry*.

"*Ocean Park #17,* 1968: Homage to Diebenkorn": Dated 9-8-95. An early draft of this poem originally opened with thirty lines that Levis later used as a discrete section of his poem "Elegy Ending in the Sound of a Skipping Rope" (in *Elegy*).

"Threshold of the Oblivious Blossoming": Dated 6-8-95

"God Is Always Seventeen": See the Afterword.

ACKNOWLEDGMENTS

The American Poetry Review: "The Worm in the Ear"

Blackbird: "The Space"; "Ghost Confederacy"; "*La Strada*"; "A Singing in the Rocks"; "The Necessary Angel"; "Elegy with a Darkening Trapeze inside It"; "God Is Always Seventeen"

Field: "Threshold of the Oblivious Blossoming"

Great River Review: "Ghazal"

Miramar: "New Year's Eve at the Santa Fe Hotel, Fresno, California"

The New Yorker: "Gossip in the Village"

Poetry: "Twelve Thirty One Nineteen Ninety Nine"; "*Ocean Park #17,* 1968: Homage to Diebenkorn"; "Make a Law So That the Spine Remembers Wings"; "François Villon on the Condition of Pity in Our Time"

Quarterly West: "Idle Companion"

Richmond Magazine: "Poem Ending with a Hotel on Fire"

The Southern Review: "In Theory"; "Elegy for the Infinite Wrapped in Tinfoil"; "Col Tempo"; "If He Came & Diminished Me & Mapped My Way"; "Anonymous Source"

Spillway: "Carte de l'Assassin à M. André Breton"

The Best American Poetry 2014 (Scribner, 2014), edited by David Lehman and Terrance Hayes: "Elegy with a Darkening Trapeze inside It"

Thanks to Bruce Boston, Christopher Buckley, Carol Muske-Dukes, Alex Long, and M.L. Williams for their help in locating poems.

Special thanks to Gregory Donovan, Mary Flinn, Anna Journey, Gregory Kimbrell, Emilia Phillips, Joshua Poteat, Amy Tudor, John Ulmschneider, and the Special Collections and Archives division of James Branch Cabell Library at Virginia Commonwealth University.

Thanks also to Sheila Brady, Nicholas Levis, Philip Levine, and Jeffrey Shotts.

AFTERWORD

After Larry Levis's death in May 1996, his sister, Sheila Brady, asked his oldest friend, former teacher, and lifelong mentor, Philip Levine, if he would be willing to edit a posthumous collection of Larry's poems. Levine agreed, and he asked me if I would help him look through what he'd been told was a significant amount of unpublished work. This posthumous collection became the book published as *Elegy.*

I had known Larry Levis since I was eighteen years old, when he first introduced me to Philip Levine, and he had become my closest friend in and out of poetry. Except for Levine, who knew Larry's work more intimately than anyone, I felt that I had an unusual perspective on these unpublished poems, as Larry was in the habit of sending copies of his poems to me, Phil, and other friends for comment long before they would appear in journals or in books. He would also send his friends a typescript copy of each new book as he was assembling it. I had agreed to help Phil in whatever way he needed, and not long after, we both received identical boxes filled with copies and drafts of Larry's poems. For the most part, this work had been pulled from Larry's computers in his office at Virginia Commonwealth University or found among his papers in his home office. Mary Flinn and Greg Donovan—founders of the superb online journal *Blackbird* and Larry's close friends and colleagues—as well his former student and friend Amy Tudor all worked to find every unpublished poem available. What we found, as Levine mentions in his introduction to *Elegy,* were multiple drafts of many of the poems, some of which were clearly unfinished; yet others seemed remarkably finished. Larry's friends at VCU had been, in my view, heroic in assembling the most complete and final versions they were able to find or construct from his many drafts; at times, they had even tried to include the revisions they'd found scrawled on scattered Post-its and other notes left on his desk.

I recognized a few of the poems in the box as having come from the period when Larry lived in Utah (1980–1994), and they'd clearly been pulled off the computer he'd brought with him from Salt Lake City to Richmond. A few other poems were originally part of a manuscript he'd sent me called *Adolescence,* but were later dropped as that manuscript became the book *Winter Stars,* published in 1985. Yet, to me, the most astonishing thing about looking at these poems gathered in their huge cardboard box was that the great majority—nearly two hundred pages—had been written since *The Widening Spell of the Leaves,* published in 1991. This was almost entirely new work.

The process of working on *Elegy* was difficult for Phil and for me too; it felt emotionally charged and—to me, at least—psychologically daunting. I believe that Levis was the poet Levine admired most of all other contemporary poets, yet he was also as much a son to Phil as he was a protégé, as much an irreplaceable friend as an admired poet. For the first few months, every time Phil and I tried phoning one another to talk about the poems we'd been reading—well, we simply couldn't do it; we couldn't talk about this impossible task. In order to talk about some selection of Larry's poems, we first had to admit that Larry was dead. It took almost five months before we could actually have our first conversation about the work itself. Finally, over that next nine months, *Elegy* began to take shape.

Levine had a clear idea of how he wanted to present Levis's work, and that was to include a group of the shorter, more lyrical pieces we had found and to set them alongside the sequence of longer "elegy" poems, which were somewhat similar in style to Levis's late work in *The Widening Spell of the Leaves.* Yet, as we looked through the poems, it was clear that there were also many longer poems that were distinct from the "elegy" poems and that stood apart from that sequence. Because it was impossible for reasons of space to include those poems also, we set them aside and, with two exceptions, included only those nine poems that were clearly meant to be part of the "elegy" sequence. Almost all of those longer, operatic, and at times wildly ambitious poems necessarily held back from *Elegy* are collected here for the first time in *The Darkening Trapeze.*

Included also in this collection is a poem with a fascinating history, "Poem Ending with a Hotel on Fire," which I have always believed was meant to be the tenth of Levis's "elegy" poems. Some of the "elegy" poems had been titled, in their early incarnations, "Poem with . . ." instead of "Elegy with . . ." I believe that "Poem Ending with a Hotel on Fire" was meant to complete the cycle of ten elegies Levis had been working toward in order to create his own *Duino Elegies,* his own *The Book of Nightmares.* Sadly, the final page of "Poem Ending with a Hotel on Fire" had been dramatically X-ed out by Levis, with an indecipherable revision scrawled down the margin alongside the X-ed-out typescript. None of us—all of whom had read Levis's cursive for twenty years or more—could read the revised version. Levine, with regret, decided we couldn't publish the poem, as we had no way of knowing what Levis had intended for the final draft. Remarkably, only a month or two after the publication of the book *Elegy,* a videotape of Levis reading "Poem Ending with a Hotel on Fire" just two weeks before his death was made available to Mary Flinn. This reading is posted for viewing at *Blackbird,* which also holds a wealth of essays and commentaries about Levis's poetry. The version of the poem that Levis read on the video was the final, revised version we had been looking for. If this final draft had been available at the time, I might have argued to publish two separate books of Levis's poems—one volume of the ten elegies, and a second volume containing the shorter poems in *Elegy,* along with a dozen or so of the longer poems now collected in *The Darkening Trapeze.*

For me, one of the most fascinating aspects of editing *The Darkening Trapeze* was to be reminded again in Levis's poetry what I'd already learned from a lifetime of conversations with Larry—that he was profoundly influenced by twentieth-century painting and photography and by world cinema as well. Fellini's influence permeates the poem "*La Strada,*" and the haunted presences of Surrealist painters and writers echo throughout Levis's wry poem, "Carte de l'Assassin à M. André Breton." Yet these are only two examples. In his earlier poetry, Levis celebrates and engages, in some of his finest early work, the paintings of Caravaggio and Edward Hopper, as well as the remarkable photographs of Joseph Koudelka. Still, in the poems of *The Darkening Trapeze,* it is the influence of the English painter Francis Bacon that feels to me most constantly present and most powerfully resonant.

In the spring of 1973, Larry and I were both living in Iowa City and saw each other nearly every day. After the release of Bernardo Bertolucci's *Last Tango in Paris*—and its accompanying artistic and cultural shock waves—Larry and I would often return to one of our favorite conversations about the film: the ways in which the film's opening credits (with its voluptuous, smoky score by Gato Barbieri) had so remarkably used two of Francis Bacon's paintings, *Double Portrait of Lucian Freud and Frank Auerbach* and *Study for a Portrait,* not only to establish the visual palette for the film but also to set the stage emotionally, and to foreshadow the drama of the story to follow. For Larry, this seemed to provide poetic instruction as well, offering the beginnings of a much broader range of narrative possibilities that he would later employ; it was then, I believe, that Larry began to look for a more highly charged emotional valence in his poems. In my view, he continued this same reinvention of narrative strategies throughout the course of his poetry, honing it in the final poems we see in the book *Elegy* and, now, in *The Darkening Trapeze*. Many years later, Larry sent me a clipping about Bacon's influence on *Last Tango in Paris,* from an interview with Bertolucci; it was a piece that seemed to Levis a confirmation of our talks, and it struck me that Bertolucci's reflections could easily stand as an *ars poetica* for Larry's late poems:

> When I decided to make the movie, I took Vittorio Storaro [Bertolucci's cinematographer] to see a Francis Bacon exhibition. I showed him the paintings, explaining that this was the kind of thing I wanted to use as my inspiration. The orange hues in the film are directly influenced by Bacon. . . . I then took Marlon Brando to see the same exhibition, and I showed him the paintings that you see at the start of the film, *Portrait of Lucian Freud,* and *Study for Portrait of Isabel Rawsthorne.* I said to Marlon, "You see that painting? Well, I want you to recreate that same intense pain." That was virtually the only direction I gave him on the film.

Individually, in the spring of 1975, Larry and I both went to New York to see the astonishing Francis Bacon show at the Metropolitan Museum of Art, afterwards exchanging now-lost postcards from the show. What I have returned to often while reading the poems of *The Darkening Trapeze* is the recognition that, even as his stylistic virtuosity reached its most dazzling peaks, the hues of Levis's final poems repeatedly first flame then darken, often as if his speakers have been afire—a common trope in his late work—and are then slowly quenched by their pain.

After I had completed editing this collection, I decided to ask Mary Flinn, Greg Donovan, and Amy Tudor if they might offer some recollections about their original work gathering Levis's poems for that initial box of poems, especially as this took place so soon after his death. Tudor's response led to a realization that there was a final poem—most likely the single last poem Larry ever completed in its entirety, a poem that had not been included in the original group of poems in that box—a poem that I had never seen. Amy recounted this story:

> Mary explained the system they'd started and then we worked together for a bit, talking here and there. Our goal was to try to decide which had been the

most recent draft of a poem, either because the piece was dated in some way or because it showed a progression of some sort that seemed a newer version of the piece. I recall thinking that what we were going to be trying to do was attempt to parse and reconstruct Larry's thinking process, his creative process, and how sometimes following a conversation with him could get a bit mysterious, so this seemed a hopeless task. But that's what death gives you, I've come to think . . .

I started on the stack of drafts of the poem that would eventually become "Elegy with an Angel at Its Gate." I laid the drafts out on the table like cards or puzzle pieces and read, and read, and read. I looked for dates first, then for significant additions ("longer equals later" seemed a good rule of thumb, at least to start), then any word changes. If there was a line that matched a previous draft but which Larry had done freehand work on (crossing things out, rewriting), you could safely assume (if any of the assuming is safe) that the handwritten changes were likely a later draft. It was part logic, part instinct, part familiarity with Larry's voice in his notes to himself. Sometimes he would have random comments in the margins or on slips of paper. Some were incredibly funny. It was strangely like spending time with him while simultaneously making me miss him more.

I did the best I could on the poem. I did the best I could on all of it. Then I read a poem he wrote about Nick—I think it was called "God Is Always Seventeen"—sitting by itself in a single draft. It was clearly recent because it had in it the darkness I'd seen in him all winter, something that was sort of gray-coated and not at all like the vaguely amused and wry face he presented most of the time. He wrote heavy poems, but he did not despair. This poem had an edge of that to it, and it was lonely and full of grief, and honestly, it made me too sad to go on with the work for that day. I ended up sitting and talking to Mary on the couch for a while instead and then going home.

I immediately wrote to Mary Flinn, but she had no memory of seeing the poem. At last, Tudor found a copy of it on files from an old computer, where she'd happened to save a copy for herself. Out of the blue, we had the concluding poem for *The Darkening Trapeze.* In my view, it is without question the final piece Levis finished, the poem he'd clearly intended to use as the last poem of his next collection.

A few years after *Elegy* was published, Sheila Brady asked Levine if he would also edit Levis's *Selected Poems.* But the editing of *Elegy* had come at a profound emotional expense for Phil, and he suggested to Shelia that she ask me to edit the *Selected Poems,* which I did. In the fall of 2010, a conference, *Larry Levis: A Celebration,* was held at VCU to celebrate the acquisition of a superb and varied collection of Levis's papers by the Special Collections and Archives division of James Branch Cabell Library. It was at this conference that Sheila asked if I would consider editing a collection of Levis's uncollected poems, as she knew I felt strongly that there was an enormous body of astonishing work still left to be published—work that only a few people had ever seen. At first, however, I said no, admitting that I felt it would be too wrenching a project. I suggested several poets who might take on the editing of the uncollected poems, but Sheila said that she would simply prefer to wait until I was ready, as she knew that, at some point, I would be. Of course, she was right. I've titled this collection *The Darkening Trapeze: Last Poems,* and it pleases me that these last poems of Levis's are no longer lost.

I continue to believe that poetry remains one of our most vital reservoirs of reflection, solace, and outrage within a world replete with horrors. Levis's poems help to remind us of our daily and necessary struggle. I see in the poetry of the poets of my own generation—as well as in the poems of the poets of the next—the lasting influence of Levis's extraordinary work. I feel the remarkable poems in this collection will now add to the conviction of many of us that Larry Levis was one of the truly major American poets of his time.

—DAVID ST. JOHN

LARRY PATRICK LEVIS was born in Fresno, California, on September 30, 1946, and grew up on his parents' ranch in Selma, California. He attended Fresno State College (now California State University, Fresno), earning a BA degree in English in 1968. It was there he met Philip Levine, who was to become his mentor and lifelong friend. After receiving an MA degree from Syracuse University in 1970, where he first worked with Donald Justice, his mentor also at Iowa, Levis taught for two years at California State University, Los Angeles. He then moved to Iowa City, where he took his PhD in Modern Letters. Levis's first volume of poems, *Wrecking Crew,* won the United States Award of the International Poetry Forum in 1971 and was published in 1972. His second collection, *The Afterlife,* was the 1976 Lamont Poetry Selection of the Academy of American Poets and published in 1977. In 1981, *The Dollmaker's Ghost* was selected by Stanley Kunitz as a winner in the National Poetry Series. Levis's fourth collection, *Winter Stars,* appeared in 1985, and his fifth book, *The Widening Spell of the Leaves,* in 1991. A collection of his fiction, *Black Freckles,* was published in 1992, and a posthumous volume of his prose on poetry, *The Gazer Within,* appeared in 2000. Over the course of his career, Levis was awarded the YM-YWHA Discovery Award, three fellowships in poetry from the National Endowment for the Arts, a Fulbright Fellowship, and a fellowship from the John Simon Guggenheim Foundation. He first taught at the University of Missouri (1974–1980), then at the University of Utah (1980–1994), where he served as Director of Creative Writing. He began teaching as professor of English at Virginia Commonwealth University in 1992 and was living in Richmond, Virginia, at the time of his death from a heart attack on May 8, 1996, at the age of forty-nine. *Elegy,* a posthumous collection of poetry edited by Philip Levine, was published in 1997. *The Selected Levis,* edited by David St. John, appeared in 2000.

The text of *The Darkening Trapeze* is set in Adobe Garamond. Book design by Rachel Holscher. Composition by Bookmobile Design and Publishing Services, Minneapolis, Minnesota. Manufactured by Versa Press on acid-free, 30 percent postconsumer wastepaper.